Sightseers into Pilgrims

Sightseers into Pilgrims

A Sampler
of
Contemporary
Christian
Poets

Edited, and with an Introduction by
Luci Shaw

TYNDALE HOUSE PUBLISHERS
Wheaton, Illinois
Coverdale House Publishers Ltd.
London, England

Photography: Walter Danylak
Cover photo: George Hess
Design: Gardner Hutchins

Library of Congress Catalog Card Number 72-97656
ISBN 8423-5886-2

Copyright © 1973 by Tyndale House Publishers, Wheaton, Illinois

First printing, April, 1973.

Printed in the United States of America.

Acknowledgments

The American Poet, "Gustatory," by Jene E. Beardsley. Used by permission.

The Banner, "Eutychus," by E. W. Oldenburg. Copyright © 1972. Used by permission. "Name," by Cor W. Barendrecht. Copyright © by *The Banner*. Used by permission.

The Christian Century, "Sister Bertha," by Jeanne Murray Walker. Copyright © 1969, Christian Century Foundation. Reprinted by permission from the January 29, 1969 issue of *The Christian Century*.

Christianity Today, "After the stroke," by John Leax. Copyright © 1972 by *Christianity Today*; used by permission. "Exile," by Evangeline Paterson. Copyright © by *Christianity Today*; used by permission.

Eternity, "Spring pond," and "May 20: very early morning," by Luci Shaw. Used by permission.

His, "Pine cherished," by Stephen Mosley. Copyright © 1971 by *His* magazine. Used by permission.

Interest, "Coming home," by Robin Shaw. Copyright © October 1972. Used by permission.

Ktaadn, "Greenly let me go," by Chad Walsh; "The current," by John Leax, used by permission of *Ktaadn* pamphlets; "My father's acres," by John Leax, used by permission.

Harold Shaw Publishers, "Royalty," by Luci Shaw. Reprinted from *Listen to the Green*, copyright © 1971. Used by permission.

Somewhere a Child Is Crying, "Word to world," by Cor W. Barendrecht. Copyright © 1971 by Cor W. Barendrecht. By permission of the author.

Spirit, "Fatherhood is a school of humility," by Chad Walsh. Copyright © *Spirit*. Used by permission.

Chad Walsh, "Rejoice in the basements of memory," from Chad Walsh, *The Unknowing Dance*, Abelard-Schuman, London, New York, Toronto; copyright ©1964 by Chad Walsh. By permission of the author.

The Westminster Press, "Perhaps the Socrates he never read," and "I will sing a new song unto the Lord," from *The Psalm of Christ*, by Chad Walsh, The Westminster Press. Copyright © MCMXIII, W. L. Jenkins. Used by permission.

Contents

Introduction / 11

E. W. Oldenburg
    In Canterbury Cathedral / 18
    Eutychus / 19

Beth Merizon
    The higher grace / 24
    Night bloom / 25
    Reception / 26
    White peonies / 27
    Morning / 30
    Oxalis / 31

Stephen Mosley
    Over and in / 34
    Prized / 35
    Praise Him / 37
    Pine cherished / 38
    Glorify, glorify / 39

Sandra R. Duguid
    Perspective on St. Joseph's Day / 42
    Spring stanzas / 43
    The tearing veil / 44

Jene E. Beardsley
    Gustatory / 48

Claiming the strange familiar / 49
An answer to Arcite's question / 50
Hopkinesque / 51
Avernus: safe conduct / 52
Apparition at Crossfield / 54
Adam at the wheel / 54
Advice for the calendar / 55

Marilee Melvin
Softly, softly / 57

Mark C. Bender
Once / 59

Robin Shaw
Coming home / 62
Real woman / 62

Cor W. Barendrecht
Word to world / 66
Name / 68

Elva McAllaster
In hunger's hunger / 73
Like this / 74
Midsummer night: Painswick / 74

David Bellinger
The devil is trying / 78
Picture of a picnic / 78
John the Baptist / 79
Ice cube / 79
If the soul could fit in one brain cell / 80
I feel like a fish / 80

Christi Cutbirth
>Sometimes / 82
>Waiting / 83
>Alpha, or Omega? / 83

Jeanne Murray Walker
>Sister Bertha / 86
>She did / 86
>Look at her now / 88
>Morning in April / 89
>Holy night / 92
>From dust to dust / 93

Chad Walsh
>Rejoice in the basements of memory / 96
>Why hast thou forsaken me? (Psalm 22:1) / 97
>Thou art he that took me out of the womb.
>   (Psalm 22:9) / 98
>My seed shall serve him. (Psalm 22:31) / 101
>Greenly let me go / 103

Luci Shaw
>Spring pond / 106
>Hungary, a memorial / 107
>Royalty / 108
>Cover story / 109
>The groundhog / 112
>On reading a travel magazine / 113
>"he who would be great among you..." / 114
>May 20: very early morning / 116

Robert Siegel
>Snakesong / 120
>Air field / 122

Wilma Gehret
    Of chapels and cathedrals / 124

Evangeline Paterson
    Dilemma / 126
    Deathbed / 127
    Miss Peewit / 130
    Exile / 132
    Reflection / 133

John Leax
    My father's acres / 136
    Poem lapsing into prayer / 137
    The current / 138
    After the stroke / 142

Introduction

In a recent letter, writer Tom Howard asked me if, as a poet in (to) the Christian world I did not feel something like "a seamstress in a nudist camp." The question made me laugh, but it is a valid one. Large segments of our civilized population, including many devoted Christians, can ascribe no useful function to poetry. They feel instinctively that poets should be doing "something constructive" rather than wasting time in such an esoteric endeavor as putting words together in clever and abstruse combinations. Surely, they feel, the same things could be put in "plain, sensible prose that anyone can understand."

This is a common view, but a limited one. And here Dr. Howard's analogy may prove useful. My answer to his question was "No, I don't feel like a unemployed seamstress. There are some people who *like* nice clothes, well made, with an eye to beauty." Perhaps the "bare" truth of factual prose can be compared to the unclothed human, and poetry to the splendid robe which warms and enhances and tells the real truth about the body. Margaret Avison early discovered that "poetry could utter what understanding could not penetrate." And it is to demonstrate this, and to clothe some truths, that I have collected some of the works of the nineteen Christian poets represented in this volume.

These poems are for those who are in the process of a discovery: that God is powerfully at work. That He not only brought into being a world of magnificent order and exotic diversity, of beauty and interest and complexity, but that He is also bringing into focus in twentieth-century life the knowledge that all truth and all beauty originate in Him and are observable today in a thousand overwhelming ways. And what about the things we cannot see? I love Edith Schaeffer's exposition of the Bible verse "For by him were all things created . . . visible and invisible." She exclaims, "All things! Invisible! The things I know are there, but cannot see — wind and gravity, atoms and electrons, oxygen and sound waves." And we can add scores of other intangibles and unseeables.

I hope the poems in this book will act as lenses to bring closer and clearer some of the things that make humanity meaningful — the visible and invisible things which really hit us hard, with a sting and a thump that wake us up. Things like new life, and nature, and death, and human relationships and relationships with God; small details in the picture that give the whole view a new logic; symbols that satisfy our human appreciation for comparisons and parallels.

Some of you who read these poems (pause, concentrate, read and skip, examine, sniff, sift, disagree, pick up and put down, re-read, ponder, exclaim, enjoy, savor, share) will have developed already the habit of poetry. Some will discover (I am praying for it) for the first time, how poetry can add a new dimension to experience and understanding. To you I would offer some concrete counsel:

1. Read a poem through. If at first its meaning escapes you, read it again. No good poem will yield itself to you in one reading. Poetry requires more sensitivity, more concentration than prose, and some poems will take more time than others. Sometimes a poem will seem to open gradually to the reader, like a flower. Don't be impatient. Look at one petal at a time. Smell it; enjoy it. There are rewards.

2. Draw all you can from a metaphor or an analogy. If you see yourself in the fish in David Bellinger's "I feel like a fish," apply all that you know about water, and fishnets, and seaweed, to understand how he felt when he wrote the poem. You may even discover something in the poem's image of which the writer himself is not aware. This is especially true of universal symbols which have different levels of meaning.

3. A good poem comes alive when it is *read aloud*. This is because rhythm and breathing are such integral parts of the poetic process. And reading aloud forces you to find and understand the points of emphasis and construction which in

turn may quicken whole sections of the poem into their true meaning for you.

The poems in this book demonstrate diversity in about as many ways as the authors are diverse: the young and not so young, the well-established and the newly-involved in poetic effort, the male and the female (an almost equal number of poets of each gender are represented), and varying political, religious, educational and cultural backgrounds directly affect the ways and words of what is written. And the poems themselves differ: short, long, straightforward, oblique, rhymed, free, implicit or explicit in their expression of truth.

In the first poem in the book, "In Canterbury Cathedral," William Oldenburg tells how the two words, "our Lord," cemented a random group of sightseers into travelers in a common pilgrimage. The mortar for each building block of this book (each poem with its different weight, feel, shape, size, color), cementing "diverse motley stones," is the unifying belief in a potent, pervasive, actively self-revealing, redeeming God. Perhaps it is with this "mortar" that some readers will be radicalized from the aimlessness of a life of existential tourism, or that the goal of their pilgrimage will be redefined and reaffirmed.

Luci Shaw
West Chicago, Illinois

E. W. OLDENBURG was born in Muskegon, Michigan, in 1936. He earned a B.A. from Calvin College in 1958, an M.A. from U. of Michigan in 1959 and a Ph.D. from the same institution in 1966.

Since 1965 he has taught English at Grand Valley State College, Allendale, Michigan, where he is currently an associate professor and chairman of the English Department. He has been writing poetry with some regularity since 1967 when he was "forced into it by agreeing to teach a creative writing course." Since that time it has become his addiction. He has published poems in *Four Quarters, Amaranthus, For the Time Being, The Brown Penny Review* and other magazines. His work has also been included in several anthologies: *Midwest Poetry* and *Modern Michigan Poets*, among others.

In Canterbury Cathedral

On a day sweet with April showers
the safe tires of our tour bus
had sung us south from London,

Sightseer pilgrims, cameras slung,
no need or time on patient plodding
horses for long diverting tales.

We stood at last at Beckett's shrine,
lost in architecture and dates,
confused by Norman and Gothic.

Our ancient tiny guide seemed shrunk
into his suit, dwarfed by his clothes
as we all were dwarfed by time.

His small precise English voice went on:
pronounced "Our Lord," and the words
fell on us like a benediction.

"Our"—incredible assumption of union
offered in passing to American strangers,
mortar for diverse motley stones.

Time and blood and history redeemed
from meaninglessness: two words
turned sightseers into pilgrims.

Eutychus

Eutychus saw light beams leap
From shining eye to eye
Across the wide room;
The lamps flared and exulted
As Paul talked on and on.
Images jumped from his tongue
Like flames from flaring wicks:
Panting runners racing,
Soldiers struggling into armor,
The rude cross, the empty tomb.
Eutychus saw wide eyes widen
As Paul's images spread
From concentrated points
To conceptual pools
Of light they loved,
Widening to flood all the world:
Of the attributes of love,
And of what love is not,
Of life, of what life is not,
Of life real, of life eternal,
Of life snuffing out death
Like a dark candle.

Eutychus in his window
Was wedged between the light
And the black Troas night;
Between his shoulder blades
The sharp window frame
Cut him in half: one ear
For the voice incessant

Speaking of life in pools of light,
One ear for voices from the dark:
A sailor's curses rumbling
Up like thunder from the harbor,
A woman's tipsy laugh,
Lilting, lingering, promising...
Life trembled and sang in the dark,
Stung in the night air with a bite of salt
From the sea that brought Helen to Troy.

And then the voices merged
For divided Eutychus—
The lights began to blur—
He dreamed his own dream,
United Eutychus dreamed his dream,
A wide-screened dream of youth,
Himself cast as Romantic Hero,
Fighting Achilles with Hector,
Putting on the whole armor...
Hacking beside Peter in the garden,
Winning first prize in the race,
Rescuing Helen (their love
Pure, of course, though she
Kissed him for reward), himself
Debating Pilate, rescuing Christ
From the mob, fighting Pharisees
With Paul, swashbuckling on a quest
For Immortal Life, like Jason's quest
For the golden fleece; Eutychus,
The one-man Church Militant,
Whirling-dervish force for right...
Just before he fell
His eyes half opened...

The lights were all whirling, whirling...
The night air half woke him
As he plunged, but then...
He was in the sea, diving
For Mycenaean treasure
In the Aegean...swimming
The Hellespont...swimming,
Swimming easily...floating,
Floating...until the earth
Struck him roughly—
Stamped his breath out.

When he awoke he seemed
To come from a deeper
And more silent dark
Than any he had known,
A dreamless dark
With no night sounds
Of cricket or distant owl;
No trumpet fanfare
For his grand reentry,
And no choirs of angels,
Only the quiet pool of light
And the circles of known faces
Breaking slowly into joy.
He had his own life back.
Not his gaudy life of dream,
But his common life of the real,
Life real, life eternal, his own life.
Really an everyday miracle
Without sound of rushing wind.
Eutychus, in the upper chamber
Saw the tongues of flame burn steady.

BETH MERIZON is a graduate of Calvin College and spent summers in Champaign-Urbana and Ann Arbor, where she received a summer Hopwood Award in poetry. Her home town is Grand Rapids, Michigan where she works as associate editor of *Christian Home and School*.

The higher grace

Since we're commanded to forgive,
Can forgiving be divine?
Where love is,
Forgiveness is;
And practice makes for ease.

Forgetting is another thing:

A burr once thrust against the mind
Is barbed to anchor and to cling
And many-pronged to sting
And is not loosened by the wind.

To err is human;
To forgive is, too.
Forgetting is divine.

Night bloom

Our planet has turned its back to
    the sun, bringing the gift of
    darkness.
Stars flower in the sky
While on earth, patterns bloom
    in the great earth shadow.
See how the shop windows glow
And the lights lacing the freeways!

The city seems a festival
As we coast down in from the hills.
As always, we catch our breath.
Signals wink red, wink green,
Signs ripple and wave,
Tall glass boxes gleam.

A visitor riding in from the past
    would say,
"What is the great event tonight?"
And we would reply (but gently)
"Nothing—it's always like this."

Reception

The candle throws a gentle light
Upon the darkening room:
A simple flame, like one that burned
To light the stable's gloom—

A wisp of fire to usher in
The light that lights the world;
The Day-spring from on high received,
And one small flame unfurled.

White peonies

With style the peonies stand in their crystal vase,
Stalks deep in a cool sea.
Drawn by the suns of spring from the dark, round
　　root—
Now whorls of satin flakes cupped like the palm
　　of a hand
At whose heart rests the golden powder,
　　quintessence of peony life,
On white, most delicate standards—
An airy rosette.

Fragrant is the room's still air with something
　　of rose
And something all peony; sweet with a tart, bright
　　edge
That assails the senses
And sends the mind spinning.

Their opulence grows with the hours,
Till suddenly
(It happens in silence with no one beholding)
A pool of white petals lies silken, voluptuous still,
On the dark mahogany.

Morning

I go on padded streets;
The earth is paved with stars
That stir like foam around my feet
And muffle passing cars.

The air is still as dawn;
The wheels go whispering by,
As though some hushed communiqué
Had issued from the sky.

Oxalis

Oxalis clovers the doorstep,
Giving the house a country air.
Like a green missile it springs from the
    earth
While the zinnias labor to grow;
Where nothing was, there is something—
This eyelet embroidery design.
It spangles the catalpa stump with green
    hearts in threes.

Oxalis in the mint bed, the bergamot,
    launching a yellow star.
I pull them up and toss them
And reach for still another . . .
But something cries, Wait!

Do we want our small jungle bereft
    of the green hearts, the grace,
    the eyelet design?

STEPHEN MOSLEY is a junior at Western Illinois University where he is studying journalism. He spent a large part of his boyhood in Latin America (Mexico and Colombia) before "being submerged in the affluent culture of the United States." His parents are teachers and he enjoys "moving around, Francis Schaeffer, tennis, football, and Crosby, Stills, Nash & Young." He hopes, someday, to make realistic movies about the Christian experience.

Over and in

Fountain
breaking over our dams
discovered and undiscovered
a current to be accepted with thankfulness
no need to try and pay back
it isn't sold
We have no claims to buying much less earning
the gift
the indestructible truth embodied
Search it out, let it clean you out
let it be
salvation
Oh man under the thumb
wrestling with who-knows-what inclinations
man bouncing off the latest circumstance
Come up for the third time. Clutch
It will hold like the Earth is held
Red eyes and sputtering it's awfully embarrassing
but let it break over
and in

Prized

Rise on the Lord
for your times are failing
with the world's last wailing
Prize on the Lord
for His listening ear
that picks up the vibrating communication
sent
Rise on the Lord
no nation can embalm you
no petition can enrighteous
Rise on the Lord
for His dream of a perfect people
not perfect like the empty world lives
but perfect like the Father fully gives
and like the future He can blend
into this life's trending
Prize on the Lord
be glad
be glad to make the We in you
thicken

Praise Him

Sing around to the Lord
for He comes with the best
Praise Him for the faith that can reason
long under the hoof it's time to fly
Celebrate with a starting sigh
thankful to Him
whose clouds paint themselves
whose stars are His own pacing His own
for rain and leaf veins
such that greens the world
Praise Him for the Cleaning Up Project
in the end of time Earth
Praise Him for being beyond in perfection
and yet lying by every bleeding side
Sing with lousy voices and pimples sing
out into the heart
so easy to open
Don't sing with a Heaven purchase card
Don't sing with fear
first find what there is in praising
and jump out at the fleeting good you caught
corner of the eye try
a start toward settling
But praise Him people
for God loves His children
like we never know how
for in praising you can say
Thank-you
my God

Pine cherished

You go down the freeway till you come to
the 23rd street exit
Yea
Take the exit to Main and turn left
Yea
Go all the way down past the Food Mart
till you get to Washington overpass
Yea
get off on the overpass exit and take it to Bruckshire
Yea
take Bruckshire one block down to First
No
What?
I want to take Pine down to First
But Pine never runs into First
But I want to take Pine
You don't understand you'll never get there
that way
Look I just want to take Pine that's all
Don't you think I know where it is
Sure but couldn't you rearrange it so that Pine
will run into First
No these things are made a certain way and . . .
I want to take Pine and that's final
It just can't be done
Aw c'mon just this once I want to take Pine

Glorify, glorify

Bathe in the Lord
for His cleansing out of sickness saturation
the sickness of this dead bliss
Swim with strokes from His strength
out into the Spring Water River Rain
of One Salvation
Praise on His mountain
where our high-low lived out
steps
can find a holding everlasting
Do kindness to make Him happy
Do kindness blindly and with an unquenchable thirst
for His joy is to see us
following
Plow in the rocky and in the soft
and sow the Center of all
seed
that leads connection
Glorify, Glorify
and separate out to glorify more purely
more richly
There will always be another better grade
and it seeps in again to make us less
here
but more touching
Praise and be swiftly content

SANDRA R. DUGUID was born in Batavia, N. Y. in 1947. After receiving her B.A. from Houghton College she taught literature and composition at Nyack Missionary College. She holds an M.A. from the Johns Hopkins University Writing Seminars and is now doing graduate work in English at the State University of New York at Buffalo. Her poems have been published in *Christianity Today*, *ktaadn*, *Spree*, and in the anthology *Adam Among the Television Trees*.

Perspective on St. Joseph's Day

the swallows are returned
to Capistrano!
flown north from the pampas
to the mission at San Juan

above the clouds their wings and tail
outline bells, catch sound
suggest the ring of hatchet blades
how Nazareth's trees were hewn

down, the swallows tend their business
restore the chipped mud nests
just south of Los Angeles
and mate near them

yesterday in New York State
bearing north on seventeen
we're brought up through the southern tier
near Fish's Eddy

and watch above the black-edged snow
beige deer fill in bare hillsides
the winter of their searching gone
bend to taste new grass

this Monday morning, spring
I think of tractors plowing in the middle states;
one from Iowa, south; another, Missouri's
west; the last in Kansas

south, sewing the winter's wheat
planning row on row
Christ's trademaster evenings
planing cabinets for his home

Spring stanzas

The melting snow recombines
Giant awkward flakes
Hurl themselves against the budding lilac;
Cherry blossoms batter
Frail petals against marble

Suitcases of crocus bulbs
Rot beneath bare sunporches
Of our ancient homes;
Seeds germinate in the wet
Newspapers saved
In downtown cornerstones

Christ, when this is
Some metaphor of spring,
Show us the real and bruised
Body darkening at Jerusalem.

The tearing veil

From within the sanctuary
of the whitewashed church
I looked out the closed window
saw a starling, flying east
flown into summer's screen

Dead for days
dark breast, sides, back
circled with the soft
splintered wire

It had never imagined such panic
and aiming toward no particular inside
did not find itself, even then
half in, half out

Dying at noon
he would have swooped from blue
to no blue, the sun emblazoning rainbows
on his back

Dying toward dusk
the sun would have cast his shadow
on the inside glass
to show another starling

Wings pinned back
trying to fly forward through the screen
the bird would not have pitied, failed to pity
been saved by the other starling

The moon became memorial for that scene
I leave it for worse

Men
crucified
have closed their eyes
back some moments
as from magnifying glass
to see The Christ
bolt upright
pinned to rotting wood

They have appealed to Him
whose wreath was the black sun
who told that moons, the need for them
shall fall
have heard the tearing veil
done with dark glass
and live that inner place
where nothing bears reflection

Save The Light.

JENE ERICK BEARDSLEY was born and raised in Mount Vernon, New York. He began to write poetry seriously in his freshman year at Wheaton College where he received his B.A. in English in 1959 he has been teaching English Literature at English from the University of Illinois. Since 1959 he has been teaching English Literature at Eastern Baptist College. He and his wife live with their three children in nearby King of Prussia.

Gustatory

North in every direction, winter kills
Outdoors all taste. To word it differently,
It is as though among these fields and hills,
Yielding once sweet bite of early timothy,
Black cherry bleeding sweetly down the tongue,
And hickory kernel, the smack of autumn in
A nutshell, now that the year is not so young,
Divided sweet and salt or sharp and thin,
Under the high flame of the sun the flavor
Has been cooked all summer long out of everything.
Men walk with a different kind of hungering
From bird or beast at a time not in their favor.
The winter seasons down its unwarmed waste
Of fields and hills, but does so without taste,
With frost, like the salt of the earth that has lost
    its savor.

Claiming the strange familiar

Along the agéd highway somewhere stood
The Family Tree, whose dark, expensive wood
Slow years had forced into a crucifix and whose
Inedible moonlit fruit, without a bruise,
Swung noiselessly in the low October wind.
I did not know it then, but, seeking news
Of my lost and ancient kin, that was the kind
Of image — hard, illumined, and moved by the wind —
That in my older nights I was to find
On long walks after sundown through the mind,
And pluck, and back in my lamplit study, free
Into the ruléd lines of my poetry.

AN ANSWER TO ARCITE'S QUESTION

"What is this world?"

When one learns it is a hospital, he feels a little
    sick at first,
Angry at the staff and desiring no visitor,
Refusing meals, refusing the medicines on the shelf,
Then, worsening, develops a refusal to refuse.
    The worst,
Then, does not happen: holding still while doctors
    examine
His incarnation, he lets himself be nursed,
The mind in wheelchair, wishing neither well nor ill
    and making no demands.

Without feeling summers pass, and winters, on
    all floors;
Plants blossom and unblossom in the rooms
    (one understands,
Now, that he never really is outdoors
In his condition); in time, though timidly, the
    friends he was angry at
Dare call again, and (since they ask) his back feels
    sore
From sitting too much in one pose — and after that,
Some mid-week afternoon he is surprised to catch
    himself
Ask whether there will be flounder or salmon
For Friday night's supper, ride down the corridor
To see the new-born, pick up in the waiting-room
    at no one's suggesting
Last month's magazine and find it interesting.

Hopkinesque

> "What is all this juice
> and all this joy?"

Glory be to God for water — for morning-wet
   Wild roses fizzing with honeybees;
     For deep, meaningful oceans that ships skim;
Wringing-wet waterfalls; drinks men in summer get
   Spine-tingling from wells and reservoirs; these
     And all rivers, their flood and eddy and swim.
All things not earth, air, fire; whatever, downing
   First from heaven, washes, freshens, will by
                   spring unfreeze,
   With low, loud; sweet, salt; merry, grim;
He rains forth whose breath is past drowning:
                     Praise Him.

Avernus: safe conduct

The burning worst of hell is not the being
There exactly, but that being there
Intends to keep the fired, idle damned
From all those striking ordinary indoor-
Outdoor movements on the surface of
The world that keep a man in excellent
Condition. So, if, after an act that sends
Me to the underworld, I still can go
About my business—under the humid summer
Digging in the garden, grading a set
Of papers on my desk (that, oddly enough,
With all its work, over the star-deserted,
God-dimmed lake at evening, has been shipped
There with me, like my other personal
Effects), or (Lord, in such a nightlong fix,
The hardest thing of all) enjoying a simple

Day with daylight friends and family who
Have no idea of where I am—if I
Can volunteer to make these movements while
Involuntary dread goddamns me, then
It is perhaps, down there, like hanging quiet,
Freshly washed and ironed curtains to
Put out the glaring windows, without panic
Laying a rug upon the burning floor,
Against that brimstone odor placing, like
A breathing spell of open air, a vase
Of Queen Anne's lace and clover on the table.
It may be that tidy curtains, rug
And vase are not external trappings only,
Hiding the pitiful condition of the place,
But the very touches, homeward charm of which
Recalls, with time, the whole mind, rowing at daybreak
Toward the familiar inlet, back on earth.

Apparition at Crossfield

An error in the calendar haunts that empty lot
Against the weight of a winter sky. In a white
Smock with black smudges, like a mediaeval miller
Slowly testing his northern flour, a birch tree,
One limb held to the air, with the sensitive twigs
Of its fingers feels the quality of the falling snow.

Adam at the wheel

No law in mind, for twenty mornings I
Have passed below the green light hanging by
Its stem just over the intersection. Now,
On the twenty-first, it ripens, click, to forbidding
Red and, even before the crime of skidding
Possibly through its shine, arrests me. How
Did it know what I had in mind, and, more unnerving,
What is it signaling: "Mind" or "Don't mind me"?
My motor racing, what in my foot is this dread
Fast move I am urged to make by the light turned red
And, along the insinuating road, the curving
Wait of hurried, hissing cars behind me?

Advice for the calendar

The first snow should not fall on Christmas, not
On any of its twelve green indoor feast days, but
In difficult, rude mid-winter when the last
Fir tree, in its false rain dangerously dry,
   is cast
Outdoors with the trash and all warm Christmas
   seems,
Perhaps, like rubbish to us in our cold extremes
Looking back from among the insults of the
   ordinary year.
In actual winter, the winds true north at the
   unclear
Removal of the sun from the sky—if it snow
   first then,
We may feast once more and drink to the health
   of men
In the pure Christ coming gently to earth again.
The first snow, raising a little the lowly lay
of our land, soothing our streets at wintertide,
In general softening the blow of winter, should
   not coincide
With Christmas. It itself is a holy day.

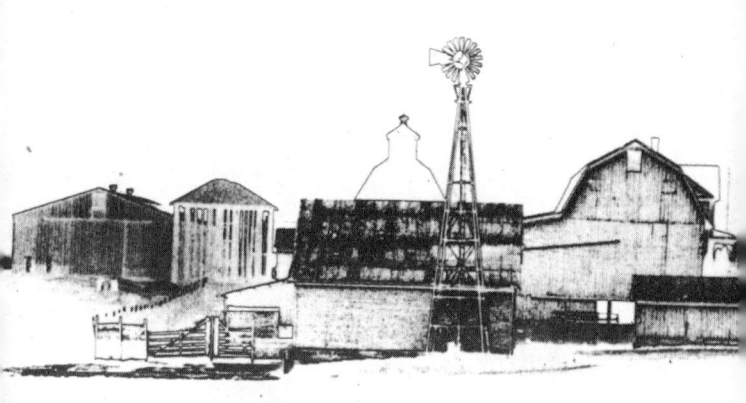

MARILEE MELVIN, Oakbrook, Illinois, was born in 1950. She has been writing poetry since her first effort, at the age of six, "The Moon." She earned her A.B. at Wheaton College in 1972 in the field of philosophy, and was included in the poetry anthology *Rappings* (Tyndale). She was mentioned in *Who's Who in American Colleges and Universities, 1972*. She is currently doing freelance writing and preparing a volume of her own poems for publication.

Softly, softly

Softly, softly,
    the truth came.
(slow-motion salt ocean waves rolling
        spreading moving inland,
   filling caves and coves and foaming white
        at breaker's edge)
No one would have seen it,
No one could have heard it,
       But there was one bright star,
       And angels sang.
(sunset over the ocean all at once too grand,
        too glorious for anything but silence;
     sunbursts into sanguine skies: purple pushes
        stone silence
      into hearts all human and humble)
The truth is hard to our hard hearts.
The best is yet to come:
      Word become flesh,
      And dwell among us.

MARK CHRISTIAN BENDER graduated from the Stony Brook School, Long Island, in 1970. He enjoys Emerson, Milton, deep thoughts, athletics. He has been writing poetry only recently, most of it concerning "aspects of memory, love, man's plight, and regeneration." He has written articles for several Christian magazines.

Once

Once
    Not so very long ago
    I was really bad n' ruined
Seemed like
    The whole world was a monster
    All the time tryin' to get just me
My life
    Was as peaceful as a mouse
    In a roomful of cats
Sound like a drag?
    It was man, it was a real drag
    Until Jesus arrived

Well I still
> Like to screw-up a lot
> But not as much as the old days

Jesus took
> The whole thing and went to work
> While I just sat back and let him

Instead of
> Always tryin' to paddle upstream
> I just settled down and followed his current

Now that's a relief
> I mean after fightin' it so long
> You gotta believe that's a relief

Anyway
> The Lord's been real patient
> Still truckin', so to speak

Someday
> He's comin' back
> And I don't mean maybe

So if
> You wanna come over some time
> Just to sing praises and stuff

You can

ROBIN SHAW is a lover of trees, "earthy" things, Joni Mitchell words and music, and sunny days. She is living in Christian community in northern Minnesota, involved in writing, design, guitar music, and finding God's will for her life.

Coming home

A door means home to me.
It's hard to come home.
Rusty hinges make the door stiff
to open, but the wood,
weatherbeaten from battle,
is strong and the doorknob
clean and round, ready to be
the tool for opening.
The keyhole is blocked so
I can't peek in but must be
ready for anything.
The knotholes in the door frame
are the wild branches I once had
but now have cut off.
I am ready to come home
through the hard door.
I have Jesus.

Real woman

My woman
will love crisp apples,
walks with the moon, sailing
ships, sunshine, the smell
of fresh hay, frogs *ribiting*.
Her house will be
earthy, tapestries

of cork and zebra skins,
moss gardens and vines
in old wine bottles.
And pots and pans from the past
will line her bedroom wall.
She'll listen to
Beethoven's Fifth
(first movement).
And her children will
be her pride. She'll let them
run naked and she'll
breastfeed them until
they're three years old.
And Jesus lives!
And she'll love the texture
of unbleached muslin
and wear
bells on her toes
and strawberry sachet
and turquoise and
patchouli oil. The golds
and greens of spring will
make her shiver. Gracious trees
praise Him!
Among antique clocks
and 16th century lace
her mate will be loved with
her heart and mind and soul
and body
and they'll walk proudly
and she'll be beautiful
in all her lovely ways.

COR W. BARENDRECHT, born in 1934 in the Netherlands, has been a prolific poet in both Dutch and English. Educated in Canada and the U.S., he received his B.A. in English and German from Grand Valley State College, Michigan. His poems have been printed in *Amaranthus*, *Credo*, *Once Again*, *The Banner*, and other magazines. As well as writing poetry and short stories he is literary editor of the *Calvinist-Contact* and in 1970 he founded a "Workgroup of Christian Writers" which published *For the Time Being*, now being published as a fine arts quarterly by the Fine Arts Fellowship. Saturday night is "poetry night" in the Barendrecht basement in Grand Rapids, and area poets find this a good sounding board for their latest work.

He is married and the father of a daughter. He has "no great models" for his poetry, though his technique has been compared with that of Robert Creeley, with the lines written in breath-groups, for easy reading aloud. He says, "The poetry written by a Christian can be a reaction to 'the Word, or to words' (Christopher Fry) . . . it can also be a reaction to silence, to the wordless situation and to sensory impressions, all of which are part of life. . . ."

Word to world

On the beach the sandy soil was soft with thirst
a digger wasp with all her energy
worked her way into a dune

In the field the red clay skin of earth
cracked like a long-deserted honeycomb
A desolate earthworm failed to break the crust

In the town a young woman in a cave
near a sandstone inn
dilated on dead, crackling straw

Nature is alive in the pulsating universe
Expansion and contraction are present
everywhere, even in human life
Sometimes in clouds we cannot push aside
it seems that even God recedes
in preparation of exertion

One child God put his arm around 280 times
in cloud formations in the crystal skies
compassionately rocking it through macrowaves
    and microwaves
polarized on planet earth

At zero hour God came
a baby on the bloody thirsty earth
with vernix on its skin
little sheep in a sundown pasture
and wrinkles on its face
little year rings of untimeliness
like summer wood in a balsam fir
and twenty billion invisible nerve cells with a
live reminiscence of heaven
and more knowledge than
100 volumes of Encyclopaedia Britannica
on the DNA of one cell string

When shepherds knocked noisily at the door
of the sepulchral sounding cave
his arms and legs swung out with a jerk
he cried an earthly roar of flesh and blood
a simple startle reaction

God spoke one small creative word
a benediction for creation

At 33, expansive wide his hands spread all around
arms thrown out wide to hug the universe
purple of passion in a sunset sky
Day without end

The Word has reached the beach, the field, the town
bloodthirsty earth of men to retrieve
chief sinners and braves
Break out of your crust
It is time to be born

Name

A name written in sand
by a child's hand;
on a San Quentin wall
by an inmate's fingernail;
in blood stains
on doorposts;
in small-print footnotes
of dissertations

A name sprinkled
on little heads;
sung over bodies
in immersion tanks

A name breathed
in wind-touched silence
of lost paradise;
carried on wings
of one-day butterflies

A name on quivering lips
of a combat soldier
alone in a foxhole;
clattering between teeth
of an aging woman;
tremored by a
protestant voice

A name remains
when writing is no more
and voices die

A name given to
what has no name

Between desire
and silence
falls a name:

Jesus, the Christ.
Paradise regained

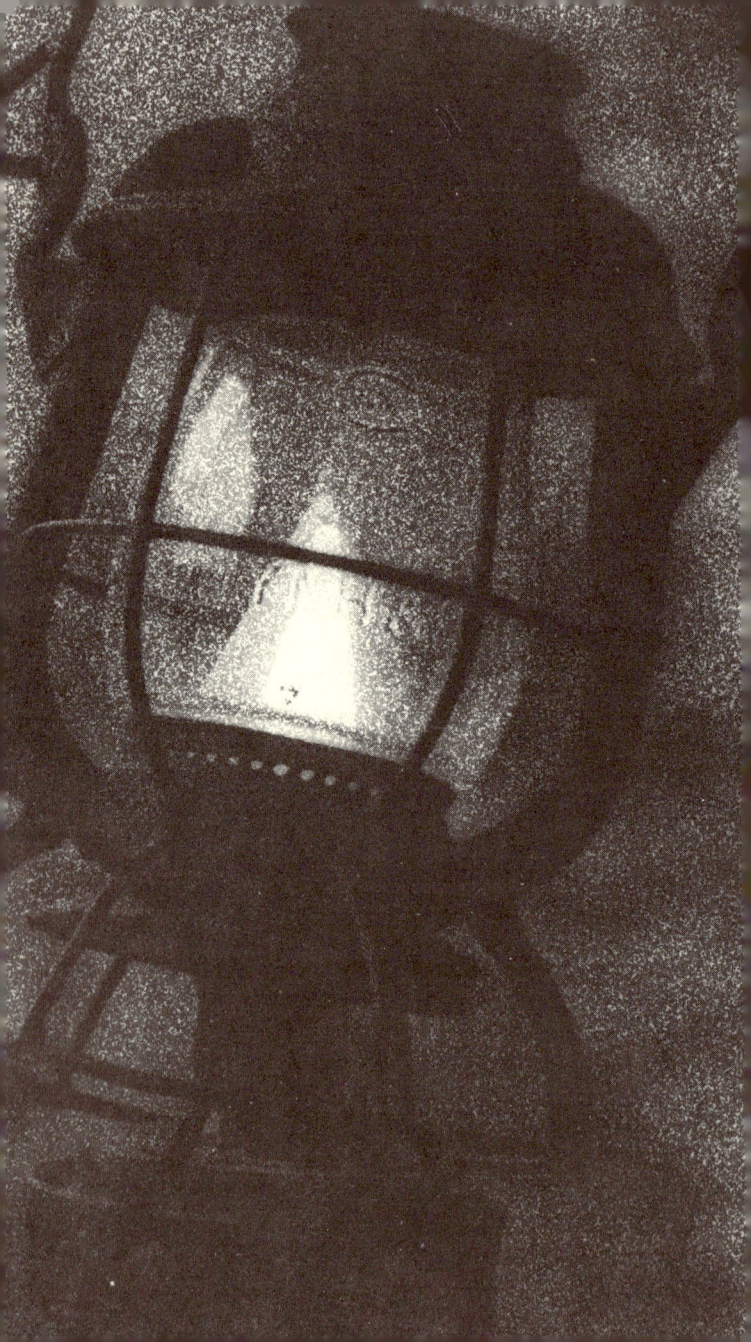

ELVA MCALLASTER is a professor of English at Greenville College and has been since 1956. Before that she was professor of English at Seattle Pacific College. For the past year (1971-72) she was poet-in-residence at Westmont College. She earned her A.B. degree from Greenville College and her Ph.D. from the University of Illinois where she was elected to Phi Beta Kappa. She has three volumes of poetry to her credit and a new fiction work, *Strettam*. She likes travel (has wandered in Israel, Switzerland, Western Europe, Canada, and Mexico) and photography.

In hunger's hunger

Being famished for cathedrals, I went out
To look for crumbs.
                This village has no hoard
Of fourteenth century glass, no Norman stone.
When Chartres was building, bison pastured here,
And foxes barked.
                Beside an asphalt road,
I saw late sun translucent through green panes
Of grape-vine leaves: saw rare imported glass.

No organs in the trees, but choirs enough.
(Do we think angels feathered, honoring birds?)

Ravenna, Venice. Have they one mosaic
More brilliant than flecked orange lilies' glow
In little alleys? Does any Gothic arch
In Rheims or Canterbury have better tilt
Of aspiration than these arching elms?

Cathedrals imitate, as best they can,
What God gave Eden; what He still gives man.

Like this

One brown oak leaf
Lies on the window ledge
With its edges serrated
Into a most delicate sculpture.

Glossy lacquered surface;
Smooth polished leaf patina.

Fawn brown,
Field brown,
End-of-autumn brown.
Immensely right,
Precisely appropriate:
Oak leaf brown.

However headlines howl
Today
It's still a world
Where oak leaves grow
Like this.

Thank God.

Midsummer night: Painswick

On such a June night in the Cotswold Hills
A cosmic nostalgia
Burns in my bones.

So Eden must have been, I think
(But more).

Gentle night air heavy with the scent
Of honeysuckle and roses.

Gentle glow
Of silvered moonlight
On haze-softened hills.

Half-awakening songs
Of dawn-awakened birds
In lulling, distant harmonies.

If this much still remains
To daze and dazzle,
Awe and overwhelm,

What did you lose us, Eve?

If these are but the fragments,
These the dregs,
What was the brimming cup,
The perfect whole?

Oh, Eden lost!
O Eve,
Forlorn, bewildered Eve.

From which station, please,
To Perelandra?

DAVID BELLINGER, Wheaton, free-lance artist and poet, contributes the following biographical data: "Prose unsays almost as much as it says. Poetry hardly unsays anything at all. I want my poem to go way over here to bloom so it won't take up anybody's room."

The devil is trying

The devil is trying to sell life insurance
on God's toll free bridge to heaven.
And as he would confess to you
if he was honest
selling life insurance
on the bridge to heaven
is the devil of a job.

Picture of a picnic

Quiet now is the memory of the people
when the symphony of the branches and the sun
is renewed a measure.
The dappled voices sing songs of light
that carry frozen faces dancing
less like green leaves on branches
than yellow leaves in the water,
rushing with the sun's current over the ripples.
Something like a breeze blows through my memory
swaying the branches of images.
Bright silence comes down the stairs
from that afternoon
and makes itself at home once more.

John the Baptist

John the Baptist said, "I feel like a closet
in which Christ just looked for a shoe lace
but couldn't find one. I thank God for a glimpse
of his face and a rough pull in the dark."

Ice cube

How like an ice cube
is my stubborn lover
poised in the pitcher
not wanting to come out.
And I not wanting to force her
pouring out the time slowly
into my glass
of tepid liquid
lacking refreshment
till she lets go at last
at no more or less tipping
but some prompting of her own
and she enters my grey ocean
with a tender splash.

If the soul could fit in one brain cell

One brain cell passes on the light.
In the cell's short life it must not fail.
Imagine God like an Indian in a canoe
paddling up your spinal cord.

I feel like a fish

I feel like a fish in
the seaweed of my parents' gospel
which sheltered me from that
shark-cruising ocean
but which also kept me from seeing
the bright strands of the fisherman's net
cleaving me from my ocean
into that great draught
pulled from the other side of the boat
flopping with my equally startled brethren
into the kingdom of the
Fisher of men.

CHRISTI CUTBIRTH is a graduate of Bethany Fellowship Missionary Training Center, Minneapolis. In 1969 she suffered a broken neck while serving as a counselor at a camp for disadvantaged ghetto children. This experience profoundly influenced her life. Her health now completely restored, she is doing colportage work in Puerto Rico. Her first poems were published during her sophomore year in high school.

Sometimes

    Sometimes
when I feel lovely
    I watch you smile
        and laugh so softly with your eyes.
I warm my soul on your quiet words ...

    Sometimes
you catch me and
        question my gaze.
But then you laugh, and we both
        wonder at the Jesus
in our love.

Waiting

Nestled sharply
   in the rich, moss-covered hills
     of my unexploration
crouches a thirsty
       dream,
impatient with the weight
     of moist earth
     and trembling both in eagerness
  and fear
to spring out
and drink of sun, wind, fresh dew.

If only I were certain it wouldn't
    die from the plunge
    I'm sure I would share it with you.

Alpha or Omega?

(chuckle)
    Lord, You're funny
and if You didn't
  laugh with me sometimes
     You know I would
die of You.

Born in 1944, **JEANNE MURRAY WALKER** attended Wheaton College (B.A.), Loyola University, Chicago (M.A.) and is currently studying for a Ph.D. at the University of Pennsylvania. In 1965 she was an Atlantic Monthly Scholar and she has published in the *Encyclopaedia Britannica,* the *Chicago Tribune, Campus Life,* and the *Christian Century.* Among her interests are tennis, a small kitten, "home arts (i.e. decorating on a shoestring)" and developing a sense of humor.

Sister Bertha

Who would guess that thin-breasted body
has wheezed Christ into three languages?
She walks down aisles to pews, an oddity
of God's redeeming grace; her sober thighs
are shut against all time and place and cause.
Who would guess her brambled hands held skies
matter-of-factly down to earth, spliced lengths
of heathen centuries to ours with their strength.

And who would guess that at night somewhere off in
a room where the loveliest thing is a fly that drones,
lying her untouched body on a mattressed coffin
she stares in the nervous dark, mad or blind,
a lover who primps her soul and thinks whole poems
into a time and place out of mind.

She did

scheme of terrible softness
sleepier than her sandals, her home's rafters,
Joseph's beard, any rough child's bed
she had heard of.

She knew the clash and scratch of dirt
on her pretty ears and eyes and mind
(don't pray that she didn't)
and subtracting them swiftly she found

terrible softness gentling her senses so
she wished on that
sweet imagined something
for a place to lay the child

who flung and spun and
pulsed like wild blood
in her memory and her mother-mind
and her transformed body.

She did scheme. But some king
blew the bugle that started her down the road
to Bethlehem, and no dream
bore up under that brutal ride.

When she came to the time
where she thought softness waited
the place of her dream had changed, and she laid
her child in the clash and scratch of dirt

but knew what she forgot to scheme
when she looked at that night's humpbacked moon
    and crazy star:
that no old dream, no rafters, no ruin matters
    much when
God needs you to hold his hand.

Look at her now

What kind of chime, anyhow, sounds
over God's eternal choirs? What bell
sings over those sonorous saints
whom all the world could not quell?

I remember my grandmother well—
a gentlewoman with thin ankles
who took me and took me and took me aside
and spoke in a singing knell
about trees which weep with real voices,
about kings and queens alive for no reason
at all—except me. She fell
wholeheartedly out of favor
with mother and father and entire worlds,
and still (dangerously) I overheard her tell
many a winter afternoon
that deeper in man than all snow is a name
to which he will answer yes. Her bell
voice became my deep name.
Look at me now. And at her:

Over God's choirs she somewhere plays
in a voice which all the world could not faze.

Morning in April

It rained last night, a mighty, gasping rain.
The buds flew open like surprised mouths.
The solemn trees turned virile green again.

Oaks sprawl above the fields, and to the south
birches fence away infinity.
The sky lies over all like a white cloth.

And the galvanized moon above the tree
is like a nail pounded with some tool
to hold the sky in place, wrinkle-free.

I sit by the window, a stage-struck fool,
watching the color of the grass, beyond
propriety. Green does not follow rules,

nor does God damn it to. Forever on
the script that moves the world are written all
the possibilities in every lawn.

I'm less than an observer. Who would call
the grass, the world, God's Will? I only know
that grass has always greened, and that oaks sprawl,
that on some mind was written this last night:

Rain fall.

From dust to dust

Cold woman earth laughs loose and free.
Her skin, like fields, taught me to sing.
I wear her sweet dust like a ring,
Desire her till eternity.
How long before she will have me?

I turn. I will seduce the sky,
The solemn mouth of endlessness
To send some word strong as a kiss.
In spirit with us all, I cry,
May some world teach me how to die.

When deserts smother fields of rye,
When waterfalls turn to stone,
Dust in my grave instead of bone,
Still men will bless blank air and try
To calculate a way to die.

I stand beneath a calm, green tree.
Oh how the mouth of sky can sing
What is and what is not, and bring
From my dumb dust a saner plea:
Before I die, God of what is,
Be love to me: Teach me to be.

Holy night

Chicago. This place may yet be Bethlehem.
Wheels unlace the streets all night,
silent on the strict ice. Listen. The hymn
of a drummer boy glistens and guts the neat
air. The shattered poor dream of God's clean
coming. The lake, shocked with cold
is torn, and the pocked buildings of Woodlawn
are torn. The ragged moon turns tired, old.

Yet briefly this place may be Bethlehem.
Chicago, two thousand years broken to peace,
waiting, wreathed and torn to be the home
of Christ. Christmas preys on this tired place.
Father, be with us in the ripping dark.
Send splints of angels, send the child, and mark
the place we cheat the centuries, where we, weary,
kneel down in praise, arise in mended fury.

CHAD WALSH is professor of English, writer-in-residence at Beloit College, and serves part-time as a priest in the local Episcopal church. Born in 1914, he was educated at the University of Virginia and the University of Michigan. He has published five books of his poetry, the most recent being *The End of Nature* (Swallow Press, 1969). He has also edited two widely used college textbooks, *Doors into Poetry* (Prentice-Hall) and *Today's Poets* (Scribner). Author of numerous books on aspects of religion, his most recent is *God at Large* (Seabury Press). Walsh's earlier book of poetry, *The Psalm of Christ*, was recently reissued by The Westminster Press in paperback.

Walsh has twice served abroad as a Fulbright lecturer—in Finland and Rome. He is married to the former Eva Tuttle, who teaches at Rockford College, and they have four daughters and six grandchildren.

Rejoice in the basements of memory

God was in touch. Stroking the holy
Extent of your arm I adored him,
Sleeping with you in his peace.

God was in sight. Seeing the sumac
That bled in the meadows of eucharist,
Daily I drank the good blood.

Hearing was God. Wind on the ripples
And laughter of girls in the attic
Sang the Commandments of God.

God was in taste. Breasts that I savored,
Dark bread that I baked in the oven
Christened the buds of my tongue.

God was a smell. Musk and the lily
Confused in the rose of a heaven
Cloyed with the fragrance of saints.

Ends of the nerves, perishing senses,
Rejoice in the basements of memory,
Kiss the emptying night.

From *The Psalm of Christ*

2   *Why hast thou forsaken me?* (Psalm 22:1)

Perhaps the Socrates he had never read,
The Socrates that Socrates poorly understood,
Had the answer. From opposites, opposites
Are generated. Cold to heat, heat to cold,
Life to death, and death to life. Perhaps the grave's
Obscenity is the womb, the only one
For the glorified body. It may be
Darkness alone, darkness, black and mute,
Void of God and a human smile, filled
With hateful laughter, dirty jokes, rattling dice,
Can empty the living room of all color
So that the chromatic slide of salvation
Fully possesses the bright screen of vision.

Or perhaps, being Man, it was simply
He must first go wherever man had been,
To whatever caves of loneliness, whatever
Caverns of no light, deep damp darkness,
Dripping walls of the spirit, man has known.

I have called to God and heard no answer,
I have seen the thick curtain drip, and sunlight die;
My voice has echoed back, a foolish voice,
The prayer restored intact to its silly source.
I have walked in darkness, he hung in it.
In all of my mines of night, he was there first;
In whatever dead tunnel I am lost, he finds me.
My God, my God, why hast thou forsaken me?
From his perfect darkness a voice says, I have not.

From *The Psalm of Christ*

12 *Thou art he that took me out of the womb.*
    (Psalm 22:9)

I will sing a new song unto the Lord.
His glory has not worthily been spoken
Though every leafy tree and blade of grass
Whispers in wind to tell his hidden Name
And though the chipmunk, charged with sun and air,
Descends into his temple under earth

To say his prayers of praise. O choirs of earth—
Leaf, scale, feather, fur, hair—proclaim the Lord!
Set in movement the molecules of air.
Let the secret word openly be spoken,
Let the high echoes answer back the Name
and breath of angels furrow through the grass.

Though he has made me fleeting as the grass,
Though mole and I are shaped of brother earth
and to the earth return—O praise his Name,
All things that breed and die. Know he is Lord
Of the amino acids, and the word spoken
To dust raised Adam's eyes into the air.

For thou hast lifted me into the air
A little while, to tread the patient grass
With moving weight, and hear thy word spoken—
Eden, Sinai, the ends of any earth,
The cross into the skull. Speak the word, Lord,
The private word into my heart: thy Name

O speak it now, and speak my hidden name
Planted in thee before birds broke the air.
Say who I am and introduce my Lord.
Ye little lives that nestle in the grass,
Slim creatures underground, wings above earth,
Be silent quickly, for the Lord has spoken.

Be clamorous quickly, for the Lord has spoken.
Sing in polyphony his public name,
Descended out of heaven to the earth.
Say, sing, chant the Name of Jesus in air
Kissing with Easter green the risen grass
That is the emerald carpet of the Lord.

The risen Lord has looked at me and spoken.
Though I am grass, he calls me by a name.
Sing high, bright air; praise him, brothers of earth.

From *The Psalm of Christ*

39 *My seed shall serve him.* (Psalm 22:31)

Fatherhood is a school of humility, it corrects
    the soul.
Girls are the best school. I have four of them.
Sometimes when I look at them, I wonder where
    I fit in.
I might claim two noses, but their owners
    wouldn't thank me
For the gift. Alison's blond hair is hers, not mine;
When Demie plays the cello I cannot contend my
    poor recorder
Prenatally put music in her. Madeline dances ballet,
A straight queen, five foot three. My six feet
    stumble at a fox-trot.
And Sarah-Lindsay, when not shaking the house with
    her declarations
Does the serene acts of compassion and love with
    the grace
Of a soul that needs no schooling, forethought,
    or prompting.
In short, here they are, and I am glad. But where
    am I in them?

I was most in them at the start. The microscopic
    miracle—
Momentary, essential—was mine four times to assist.
It was as though four times I was able to help
    open a door,
And four bright spirits, assorted, entered from
    outer space.

Now they walk the four pilgrim paths, each in her
    style.
What I have told and shown them of God is as
    transient
As the last year I could outswim Sarah in the race
    to the dock.
If they find God, or are found; if they have him,
    or rather
If he has them, it is in four separate and secret
    ways.
Those doors are not mine to open. I do not knock.

Instead let me praise the fact. In any poem I write,
In my handwriting, or the way I build a bookcase
There is more of me than in Demie, Madeline,
Sarah, and Alison. They are a revelation
Not of me, but of the other father. Glory and laud
Forever to him who has given me more than a trinity
Of bright messengers, giggling with creation's
    first dawn,
In the ballet of a water fight between the float
    and the dock.

Greenly let me go

Hold me, dear God, one inch this side of death.
Closer, closer, almost the edge
Your little finger's nail to fence it out.
Lazarus of the two estates
I'll modulate the harmony of both.

There now,
Rising and sinking in this maple's roots,
Greening its leaves
Or reddening them against a common fall,
Dyeing my sky the virgin's blue,

I am the flakes of snow,
The absolution of each leaf that fell,
The tilting globe,
Hold me a little while
Till maples green. And greenly let me go.

Born in 1928 of missionary parents, **LUCI SHAW** spent her childhood in England, Australia, and Canada. In 1953 she graduated from Wheaton College with a major in English Literature, a minor in Greek. A member of the Wheaton Scholastic Honor Society, she and her husband, Harold, live with their five children on an acre of oaks and black walnuts in West Chicago, Ill. where they operate a publishing house, Harold Shaw Publishers. Mrs. Shaw's poems have been widely published in Christian periodicals and she is the author of a volume of poetry—*Listen to the Green*. Recently she has been anthologized in several collections of modern verse, including *Adam Among the Television Trees*.

Spring pond

Look how the sun
lies on the low water!

Spread ripple-shaped he
has lost roundness

Light joined to the pond
in a fluid fusion

And I, earthy,
wed now to the high Sun

Give God a new shape
to shine in

Hungary, a memorial

We who have been
free men, owners of breath,
careless masters of our bodies,
knowing only one dimension
of the right, the strong, the happy,
gulping freedom unnoticed with
the good wine of our homeland—
we must learn now
the meaning of bars, and understand
the rhetoric of
mass-produced indictment, and intone
the litany of total restriction.
There is a numbing discipline
in undeserved blows
and a new hardness in the voices
we hear. Death
sits with us every day
in the court, in the cell.
And as we raise the cold water
to our mouths
and the hard bread and the dry few beans
and the dead soup
we are learning a new thanks—
pronouncing a real benediction.
We can tell you more about freedom
now.

Royalty

He was a plain man
and learned no latin

Having left all gold behind
he dealt out peace
to all us wild men
and the weather

He ate fish, bread,
country wine and God's will

Dust sandalled his feet

He wore purple only once
and that was an irony

Cover story

Raw earth is protective enough
to clothe itself with whatever
seeds drift by, sink,
sprout, spread a green
shade of leaves.
Even a bare rock encourages
lichen, and mosses
velvet over the death of trees.
Facts are difficult enough:
like Adam, we soften,
endlessly, our pointed naked souls
with trivialities.

Still, under the new paint
the old clapboards hold on
even though we miss the message
of weathered wood.
Age need suffer no such
amelioration. The greyed
grain and the warp and the
dark knothole
are all true and precious
even if we cringe at a
now and then splinter
in our probing finger.

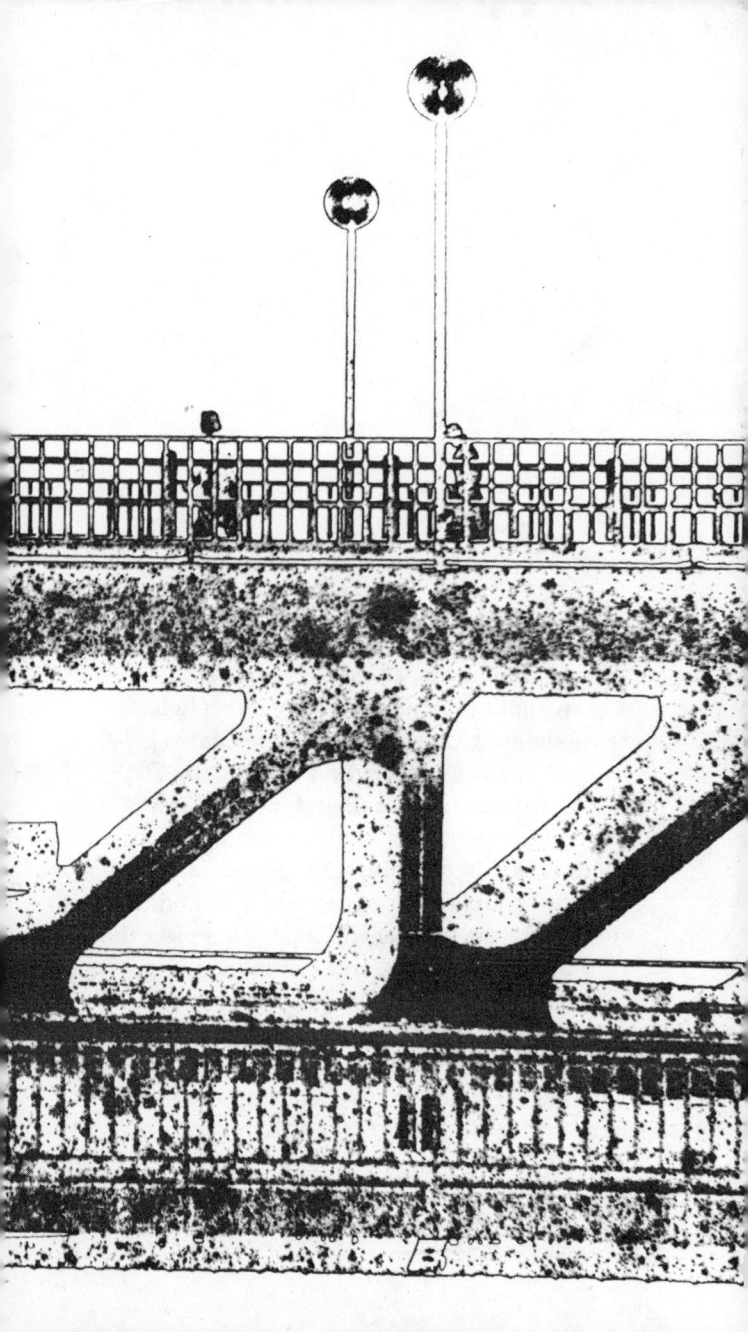

The Groundhog

The groundhog is, at best, a simple soul
    without pretension, happy in his hole,
twinkle-eyed, shy, earthy, coarse-coated grey,
    no use at all (except on Groundhog Day).
At Christmastime, a rather doubtful fable
    gives the beast standing room inside the stable
with other simple things, shepherds, and sheep,
    cows, and small winter birds, and on the heap
of warm, sun-sweetened hay, the simplest thing
    of all—a baby. Can a groundhog sing,
or only grunt his wonder? Could he know
    this new-born Child had planned *him*, long ago,
for groundhog-hood? Whether true tale or fable,
    I like to think that he *was* in the stable,
part of the Plan, and that He who designed
    all simple wonderers, may have had me in mind.

On reading a travel magazine

The phoenix' decorative flames
are about to be extinguished
in a surfeit of holy water. The Ganges
shimmers tranquilly under my chair,
reflects the convoluted tip of the
unicorn's unique horn.
Pale green bamboo shoots sprout
like haiku from the waste
basket. I open my window.
All I can hear is the warm
Tahitian rain.

"he who would be great among you . . ."

You whose birth broke all the
social and biological rules;
son of the poor who accepted
the worship due a king;
child prodigy in debate with
the temple Th.D.'s; you
were the kind who
used a new math
to multiply bread, fish,
faith. You practiced a
radical sociology: rehabilitated
con men and call girls.
You valued women
and other minority groups.
A G.P., you specialized in
heart transplants.
Creator, healer,
shepherd, story-teller,

weather-maker, botanist,
alchemist, exorcist, iconoclast,
seeker, seer, motive-sifter,
you were always beyond, above us,
ahead of your time
and ours.
      And we would like
to be like you. Bold
as Boanerges we hear ourselves demand:
"Admit us to your avant-garde.
Grant us degree
in all the liberal arts
of heaven." Why our belligerence?
Why does this whiff of fame
and greatness
smell so sweet? Why must we
compete?
Have we forgotten
how you took, simply, cool water
and a towel for our feet?

May 20: very early morning

all the field praises Him/all
dandelions are His glory/gold
and silver/all trilliums unfold
white flames above their trinities
of leaves/all wild strawberries
and massed wood violets reflect His skies'
clean blue and white
all brambles/all oxeyes
all stalks and stems lift to His light
all young windflower bells
tremble on hair
springs for His air's
carillon touch/last year's yarrow (raising
brittle star skeletons) tells
age is not past praising

all small low unknown
unnamed weeds show His impossible greens
all grasses sing
tone on clear tone
all mosses spread a spring-
soft velvet for His feet
and by all means
all leaves/buds/all flowers cup
jewels of fire and ice
holding up
to His kind morning heat
a silver sacrifice

Christ, make of my heart now
an open field
to raise Your praise

ROBERT SIEGEL took his B.A. at Wheaton College, an M.A. in the Writing Seminars at Johns Hopkins, and his Ph.D. in English at Harvard. He is currently assistant professor of English at Dartmouth College, where he serves as advisor to the Poetry Room and assists Poet-in-Residence Richard Eberhart in the poetry program. He has published poems in a number of magazines, including *Poetry, The Atlantic Monthly, Prairie Schooner, Poetry Northwest, The Beloit Poetry Journal,* and *The Christian Century.* In 1970 he received *America* magazine's Foley Award for his poem "The Rock." He is currently circulating a manuscript called *The Beasts and the Elders.* He spent most of this past year living in England and working on a second manuscript "resembling a sonnet cycle." His wife Roberta and he have three little girls and live in Hanover, New Hampshire.

Snakesong

In the green swim of trees
in the silk clothes of spring
the sparse birds
made a singing net
the small red barks

split at the green nudge.
I clung to the trunks
went under the roots
to the heart of the pull
sidled and rustled

sloughed off my skin
and waved my word
thin red fire
around the spotted
and dewed damps of life

those small numps
uncurling
twigs ticking and swelling
flames of newts
young rabbits

puffing like milkweed.
I curled round the garden
thin hose of breath
noose of the spirit
simple string

undone by everything.
This was me
before I walked a man
or made palaver
or wavered at woman

before that sweet fig
fixed my tooth
and, scotched, I sagged
to the cellar of roots
and the coiling thought

then with feet and hands
clung to the sky
moved upright as a tree
in the crooked light
found my tongue and spread
a mist over the world.

Air field

All day the great planes gingerly descend
an invisible staircase, holding up
their skirts and dignity like great ladies
in technicolor histories, or reascend,
their noses needling upward like a compass
into a wild blue vacuum,
leaving everything in confusion behind:

In some such self-deceiving light as this
we'll view the air force base when moved away
from where its sleepless eye revolves all night.
We'll smile and recollect it conversationally —
tell with what ease the silver planes dropped down
or how they, weightless, rose above
our roof. We'll pass it with the sugar and cream,

forever sheltered from this moment's sick
surprise that we have lived with terror, with pride,
the wounded god circling the globe, never resting,
that in the morning and the evening we have heard
his cry, have seen him drag his silver wings
whining with anguish like a huge
fly seeking to lay its deadly eggs.

(The "wounded god" in the last stanza is Satan in Paradise Lost, circling the earth seven times before re-entering the garden)

WILMA GEHRET of Ephrata, Pennsylvania, will graduate from Wheaton (Illinois) College in 1973. Majoring in literature with an added concentration in speech, she is a member of the literary society, Lambda Iota Tau, and the forensic society, Pi Kappa Delta. "Of Chapels and Cathedrals" was an entry in the college's Creative Arts Festival.

Of Chapels and Cathedrals

i have built cathedrals
    great towering structures
        of silence
    where i have gone alone
and listened to my heart
    (or even yours)
    drone away the hours
i have built cathedrals in minutes or less
but then cathedrals are easy to build

i am building a chapel
    my friend
(would you help me with the work)
we will need tambourines
    and songs
    and mostly
        a lot of each other
        and God

i am building a chapel
the roof may leak a little
and it will take
    a long time
        to build

EVANGELINE PATERSON supplies the following biographical facts: Born in Limavady in 1928. Grew up in Dublin as a preacher's daughter and married John Paterson (a preacher's son, which helped). Lived briefly in Cambridge when first married where her husband pursued his studies and outreach as a geographer. Since then she has lived in St. Andrews, Fife, Scotland where she is a "part time secretary and reluctant housewife who writes poetry in spite of three teen-age children." Her passions are people, modern Scottish painting, and music, from Monteverdi to the Modern Jazz Quartet. She is active in Christian Arts groups in the British Isles, organizing poetry workshops and encouraging younger artists by exhortation and example. She says, "I write with neither motive nor message but because I can't help it, and never know when or how the next poem is going to happen."

Dilemma

The water that I live in
is full of piranha
and it doesn't do
to have a bleeding heart
in this locality.

Please God
get me out of this water

or give me a shell

or teeth . . .

Just don't leave me here
with nothing
but the conviction
that piranha
are all God's children
too.

Deathbed

Now, when the frail and fine-spun
Web of mortality
Gapes, and lets slip
What we have loved so long
Out of our lighted present
Into the trackless dark

We turn, blinded,
Not to the Christ in Glory,
Stars about His feet

But to the Son of Man,
Back from the tomb,
Who built fire, ate fish,
Spoke with friends, and walked
A dusty road at evening.

Here, in this room, in
This stark and timeless moment,
We hear those footsteps

And
With suddenly lifted hearts
Acknowledge
The irrelevance of death.

Miss Peewit

Lord, forgive Miss Peewit
For the hat that she wears on Sundays.

Lord, forgive her its shape
Which is an outrage
And forgive her its color
Which is like mud
And forgive its intention
Which is to garb Miss Peewit
Suitably for a creation
Which is somehow not yours.

She has never admitted
To her heart the small and transient
And quite unnecessary violet;
She has barred her shutters

Against the sense-stealing, dangerous
Breath of the rose;
And if she should see the deliciously
Frivolous scented puff-ball
Flower of mimosa
She would think You had played a joke
In very poor taste.

Lord, forgive Miss Peewit
And prepare her gently for heaven
Where some day she is going
To have to live.

And meantime, Lord, look not
On the hat that she chooses to wear
Twice weekly to Your house
In Your honor.

Exile

Yes, it is beautiful country,
The stream in the winding valley, the knowes
    and the birches,
And beautiful the mountain's bare shoulder
And the calm brows of the hills,
But it is not my country,
And in my heart there is a hollow place always.

And there is no way to go back,
Maybe the miles indeed, but the years never.

Winding are the roads that we choose,
And inexorable is life, driving us like cattle
Farther and farther away from what we remember.

But when we shall come at last
To God, Who is our Home and our Country,
There will be no more road stretching before us,
And no more need to go back.

Reflection

I used to think—
Loving life so greatly—
That to die would be
Like leaving a party
Before the end.

Now I know that the party
Is really happening
Somewhere else;
That the light and the music—
Escaping in snatches
To make the pulse beat
And the tempo quicken—
Come from a long way
Away.

And I know too
That when I get there
The music will never
End.

JOHN LEAX was born near Pittsburgh, Pa. in 1943. He graduated from Houghton College in 1967 and received an M.A. from The Johns Hopkins University writing seminars in 1968. His poems have appeared in many periodicals such as *Christianity Today, Southern Poetry Review, Tenn. Poetry Journal,* and the *CCL Newsletter* and in three chapbooks, *A Proper Reticence, The Screen of Nature,* and *Finding the Word.* Married and the father of one daughter, he is a member of the writing faculty at Houghton College and co-editor of Ktaadn Poetry Press.

My father's acres

Like an army preparing a siege
the woods mass
around my father's acres.

They've taken the cornfields,
the neighbor's orchard and swept
across the field of winter wheat
that bowed in the wind
like a kneeling congregation.

No farmer seeking profit
from the land, my father
had no quarrel with woods.
His code read, *Love your enemies.*
He cast his lot against the grain;
he planted trees.
The dogwood, maple, hemlock
and tulips rooted
with my youth have prospered
in his soil and rise
twenty feet above his roof.

Outflanked, the woods have lost.
Ordered and in place, they shade his evening's rest.

Poem lapsing into prayer

1
The south slopes are clear
and filled with red-winged blackbirds,
but there is still more snow than grass.

2
What we planted in the fall
is shooting green from the ground
where our living rushes spring.

3
Soon the peepers will climb their slender reeds
and pipe the marsh alive.

4
Remember the faith that planted;
let this rebirth be our own.

The current

>the Genesee Valley

This is the landscape of order:
acres of corn and potatoes
split and measured
by roads disobedient
to the river's slow meanders.

Once, in a borrowed boat
I obeyed them
and under me felt
the current stronger and
further reaching
than the grip of concrete.

Mornings now, after rain,
I go out
to the edge of the field
and bending, place a finger

in the current's narrow spoor
and touch in the soil
the confirmation of my fear.

And yet, these Appalachian hills
receding an eighth of an inch a season
are not the measure of our lives.

It is the darker current,
not water,
that roars as silently as the stars
and rips the trees
from Calvary's banks
and tumbles stones before it
that replenishes the soil
and marks a man.

In it I find my proper fear
and in that fear, my life.

After the stroke

The embolism loose
from the heart
lodged in the brain
a sudden confusion of language
paralysis
and the end of speech

> As for man, his days are as grass.
> Psalm 103:15a

Beside your bed,
I cannot speak the prayer
that begs for your recovery.
The Groaning Spirit
who gives us leave to pray
withholds that comfort.
He has given me, instead,
sleeplessness,
open eyes to watch
the sweet liquid, fortified,
drip three days

into your needled arm.
My mouth stays shut.

> Bless the Lord, O my soul.
> Psalm 103:1a

It is no easy thing
to bless the Lord in Buffalo
where you lie
stroke still and dumb.

My watch is pointless,
kept only for myself.
The nurses, crisp professionals,
need neither me
nor my questions.

The heat of your room drives
me out into the street.
The 5 A.M. winter wind
is cold. Its voice,
a quick thin blade, slips
through the layered wool I wear
and speaks deep into my side
the word that alters all.

> He hath not dealt with us after our sins,
> nor rewarded us according to our iniquities.
> Psalm 103:10

In the therapy room
they held you by a belt
stood you up

and told you,
Walk.

You thought hard,
clutched the rails
and throwing your foot
like a loose shoe
stepped into the pain
and did not stop
until you'd walked it through.

But there were others there,
almost as young as you,
whose only grace
was the white webbed belt
around their waists.

> Who satisfieth thy mouth with good things.
> Psalm 103:5a

When your words returned,
they came at random,
jumped from your lips
out of context
and refused to lie down
in sentences;

but they did return.
And slowly felt your lips
and tongue divide the syllables
until, one day, dominated,
they spoke as ordered
and blessed the name of God.